DATE DUE	
JUN 1 1 2004	
JUN 2 2 2004	

BRODART.   Cat. No. 23-221

At Home in Canada

Nicole Eaton & Hilary Weston

PHOTOGRAPHY BY JOY VON TIEDEMANN

VIKING

VIKING

Published by the Penguin Group

Penguin Books Canada Ltd, 10 Alcorn Avenue, Toronto, Ontario, Canada M4V 3B2

Penguin Books Ltd, 27 Wrights Lane, London W8 5TZ, England

Viking Penguin, a division of Penguin Books USA Inc., 375 Hudson Street,
New York, New York 10014, U.S.A.

Penguin Books Australia Ltd, Ringwood, Victoria, Australia

Penguin Books (NZ) Ltd, 182–190 Wairau Road, Auckland 10, New Zealand

Penguin Books Ltd, Registered Offices: Harmondsworth, Middlesex, England

First published 1995

10 9 8 7 6 5 4 3 2 1

Printed and bound in Singapore on acid-free paper ∞

Canadian Cataloguing in Publication Data

Eaton, Nicole & Weston, Hilary
    At home in Canada

ISBN 0-670-84988-X

1. Dwellings - Canada. 2. Dwellings - Canada -
Pictorial works. I. Weston, Hilary. II. Title.

GT228.E37 1995   392'.36'00971   c94-932062-5

Book and jacket design by V. John Lee

CONTENTS

For Thor, Thor Edmond and Cléophée,
who, for me, are what home is all about
      — *NE*

For Galen
      — *HW*

To Jagan and Janaki
      — *JvT*

ACKNOWLEDGEMENTS

We are particularly grateful to the following for their invaluable help in putting this book together: Bonnie Ashby, Liza Bosnar, Maureen Boyd, Terri Clark, Irena Kankova Cohen, Jim Coutts, Karen Docherty, Jane Edwards, Arthur Erickson, Catherine Evamy, Martha Evans, Marlene Josiak, Peggy McKercher, Liz Nichol, Honour Robertson, Shirley Robertson, Terese Romer, Thecla Sweeney, Alannah Weston and Sarah White and most especially our friend and editor David Kilgour.

NE & HW

Special thanks to Nicole Eaton and Hilary Weston; Reinhold Mueller Toronto for Leica supplies; and Kodak Canada Inc. for their generous help with Lumière film.

JvT

PREFACE

Home: abode, asylum, haunt, hearth, birthplace, hospice, homestead,
place to care for and be cared for, private place, dwelling

WHEN WE SET OUT TO DISCOVER what home means to Canadians, we had a few preconceptions based on our own experience: to both of us, home was above all a place for family, but also one for private retreat and self-expression, for comfort and the preservation of much-valued traditions. We still believe this to be true, but we also found that at the close of the twentieth century the definition of family itself has broadened: it can be anything from a traditional unit of father, mother and children to an order of monks who have chosen to follow a spiritual path together, or a single person living surrounded by an extended group of friends.

Crossing the country several times, we found, as expected, a dazzling variety of homes, some traditional, some modern, some rooted in the country, others in the centre of cities, some simple, some glamorous. Unfortunately, we couldn't include them all, and so in our final selection we chose homes and the people who had made them on the basis of personal and visual appeal, uniqueness or eccentricity — and contrary to popular belief, Canada has its fair share of colourful, creative and eccentric individuals.

This is not, then, a comprehensive cross-section of Canadian homes; nor is it a book about interior design. It is, quite simply, about how some of us, in a very large country, in very different landscapes and under very different circumstances, live in our houses, use them and enjoy them.

All the people we met shared a deep attachment to and pride of place, but beyond that, few generalizations can be made. Many, not surprisingly, are visual artists who work at home, but others, in a trend that appears to be accelerating, have also chosen to blend work and home life in one space.

In some cases we went for the traditional, what some might call clichés — a cottage in Georgian Bay, a lobster feast in Nova Scotia, a cattle ranch in Alberta. But a family of artists standing in a canola field in Saskatchewan? A couple living in a converted gas station in Halifax? A reconstruction of a Chinese canal house in downtown Vancouver? We feel strongly that all — familiar or otherwise — are equally valid, equally true to the Canadian experience.

Almost all of the homes included here are entirely private.

The notable exception is Rideau Hall, which we felt belonged because it is Canada's first home, or, as one governor general described it, the nation's "living room."

As much as possible, we have tried not to editorialize but to let individuals speak for themselves — and many of them have been amazingly open about their lives, their families, their dreams.

We were lucky to be collaborating with photographer Joy von Tiedemann, whose craft and tact helped us capture the spirit of each family and the space they had created around them, whether they were formally posed or caught in passing. This book is a result of that collaboration, but, of course, it wouldn't have been possible without the kindness of the many Canadians who willingly opened their doors to us and welcomed us into their lives.

Nicole Eaton, Hilary Weston
Toronto, April 1995

AT
HOME
WITH

ALBERT

AND

CECILIA

POON

Cecilia and Albert in the front hall with Tiny.

WHEN ALBERT AND CECILIA POON arrived in Vancouver from Hong Kong in 1983 with their two sons, Edwin and Bryan, who were then thirteen and six, they all felt culturally isolated. Both children had to learn English, and there was only one other Chinese child in Edwin's class. But Vancouver has changed a lot in ten years: now half the children in Bryan's school have an Oriental background, and one can shop, bank, and get medical help in Chinese; Cecilia even says that some of the Chinese restaurants here are better than many in Hong Kong.

Albert has made a full life for himself in Canada. As well as his business interests, he relishes a good game of golf, and has discovered with gusto the Canadian wilderness, fishing and hunting with friends. The move was more difficult for Cecilia in the beginning — the independence expected of a woman living in North America was a shock for someone brought up to live a sheltered, genteel existence. Now, however, she would not go back; she enjoys the freedom of moving about on her own, taking her boys out for dinner when Albert is away or going to Seattle for the day.

The story of the magnolia tree in their back garden is a fitting allegory of the Poons' own story of putting down roots and thriving in a new land. For ten years, when Cecilia walked her dog, Tiny, around the neighbourhood, she always stopped to admire a magnolia tree that she particularly liked. About the same time that she and Albert started to build a home for themselves, the house with the magnolia tree went up for sale, so Cecilia knocked on the door and inquired whether she could buy the tree. Soon, much to

*The back of the house features
sliding screens reminiscent of
the vernacular architecture
of Sowchow.*

*Albert feeding the fish in the
pond through a door
in the kitchen.*

their neighbours' fascination, it was hoisted precariously by crane over the Poons' garage roof into their back garden, where its petals now drop gently into the pond.

Albert, who admires Japanese culture, wanted a house that was Oriental in feeling, built as it might be in Japan. Cecilia wanted a house that was easy to live in with Bryan and Edwin and Tiny. Both she and architect Bing Tom liked the old houses of Sowchow, known as the Venice of China because of its canals and water gardens. The final product was a house that presents a neutral face to the street but opens out to an inner court at the back. Because Albert preferred water rather than grass, which he felt was flat and unmoving, Bing designed the inner court as a pond which covers almost the entire back garden. There, on an island, is Cecilia's magnolia tree.

Three kinds of fish — large carp, trout and koi — flourish in the pond along with Edwin's two turtles, grown too large for his aquarium. A heron periodically lands and looks for fish, and at dusk raccoons stealthily invade the garden. To feed the fish Albert just opens the kitchen window.

The house itself is serene and composed, a mixture of Chinese artifacts and paintings and western technology and comfort. The kitchen articulates the duality of cultures with its woks and beautiful Japanese pottery dishes on one hand and a gleaming stainless-steel cook-top on the other. East meets West over bowls of rice and bean-curd soup and a carton of Kentucky Fried Chicken.

Outside Cecilia's sitting room is a small walled "feminine" garden planted with low, soft evergreens, ferns, grasses and flowering shrubs; outside Albert's study is a "masculine" garden designed around rocks, moss and pine trees. Upstairs, on the second floor, Cecilia, who is a painter and calligrapher, has a studio. On warm days, she slides open the screens and paints looking out over the pond and magnolia tree.

Nourished on a strong sense of where they have come from, the Poons seem to be blossoming in Canadian soil.

Albert relaxing in the library, which overlooks both the pond and the "masculine" garden.

Cecilia sketching in her second-floor studio, with her beloved magnolia tree as a backdrop.

Albert's custom-designed wok cook-top.

A collection of snuff bottles in a vitrine in the living room.

AT
HOME
WITH

SERGE

DESCHAMPS

AND

MONIQUE

LAWRENCE

The main living space.

SERGE DESCHAMPS AND MONIQUE LAWRENCE live with their two young sons, Marc Antoine and Olivier, in a narrow street of low-rent housing overlooking railroad tracks in St. Henri, a working-class district of Montreal. When Serge, a former contractor, bought the house in 1982, it was almost in ruins, so he went to City Hall to get a permit to renovate, only to discover that the City wanted to raze his house and others to build public housing. With an iron-jawed will, he worked on the house without a permit for four months until the City finally gave in and issued him a construction licence.

The house was originally built in 1870 by a carpenter for his own use. The small building at the back of the garden which Serge now uses as a studio was built around 1900 to house workers building the Victoria Bridge.

During the renovation, anything that couldn't be salvaged was replaced with historically authentic materials. The front and back doors, for instance, came from similar houses in St. Henri that had been torn down. At a demolition depot, Serge found the wide pine floorboards. The colours throughout the house are true to the nineteenth century: Serge carefully matched the original

17

An elaborate toy train set includes a scale model of the Deschamps house.

Herbs on a kitchen table flourish in the winter sun.

A treasured wood-burning stove is sometimes used for heating in the winter.

Serge's paintings reflect the colour palette used throughout the house.

Father and son enjoy a quiet moment after school.

OVERLEAF: Serge's studio in a shed behind the house overlooks the railway tracks.

colours found in the nooks and crannies of floorboards and window frames.

Serge and Monique are quiet, tidy people, and their surroundings reflect their personalities. Objects, paintings and furniture, which have all been "found" or made by them, create an aesthetic whole. The colours are subdued: ox-blood red, soft greens and blues. Nothing is placed at random, nothing is haphazard or gratuitous. The pine dinner-table shines, the pretty lace curtains flutter in the draught from the open door, the herbs on the kitchen window-sill catch the sun, even the shadows fall on the pine floorboards in a pattern reminiscent of a Dutch still life.

Except for a brief stay in the countryside outside Montreal in the early seventies, where they discovered their passion for renovation and tasted their first success at bringing a house back to its original state, Serge and Monique's wanderings have been confined to St. Henri and its environs. They both have a strong sense of place, and memories of childhood and courtship have rooted them in the neighbourhood. Serge was brought up not far away from where they live now, and Monique came regularly to visit relatives. Indeed, the two met in a house across the street from their own.

Serge spends most of his time painting in his studio, which is heated by a wood stove in winter. There, he can hear the trains going past on their voyages to faraway destinations. A collector of model trains all his life, he has set up in his basement twelve complete sets of trains amidst a whole village of cardboard houses made to scale.

Serge's life as a contractor is behind him. He has won many awards and prizes in recognition of the quality of his historic renovations but now wants to be thought of as an artist.

Monique likes living in the neighbourhood because she feels it's like living in the country. In the summer, she grows vegetables in a community plot nearby, and during the school year she can walk her sons to their school. She has found the time to teach herself to play the piano and the accordion, and when they have friends over for dinner on Saturday night or for Sunday lunch, she enjoys singing for them. Cooking, music and painting are her passions.

Serge and Monique have chosen a life of small pleasures, enjoyed with rare delight and intensity — and they seem more than content with it.

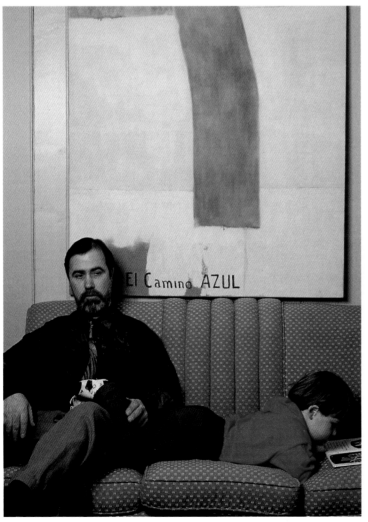

Coats for all seasons.

AT
HOME
WITH

ROBERTO
AND
LUCIA
MARTELLA

IT'S NOT SURPRISING THAT THE MARTELLA FAMILY lives in an apartment over their business: after all, Roberto grew up over his immigrant father's barber shop (complete with a barber's pole brought from his native Abruzzi, Italy) at the corner of Bathurst and Dupont streets in Toronto.

Lucia was four when her family decided in the early fifties to emigrate from Italy. Her mother soon found work in a food processing factory and her father in the Ontario Parks Department.

Lucia remembers, "You felt good at home, you felt safe, you knew what was expected of you. Family meals were an important part of these traditions."

According to Roberto, "Like all great chefs, Lucia learned to cook at her mother's knee." But in spite of her great interest in cooking, Lucia attended university, where she studied anthropology. Meanwhile, Roberto graduated from the University of Toronto in liberal arts.

In the seventies, Roberto worked in the wine-importing business, but he longed to open his own restaurant. In May 1986 he realized his dream. Grano — grain — the restaurant Roberto and Lucia have created together, combines the best of Italy and Canada, and the best of their talents: Lucia cooks, Roberto manages.

Some of the vegetables used in the kitchen are grown by Lucia's father in the garden behind the restaurant. The décor of the apartment above is all about colour cleverly used, the *objets d'art* are engaging to the eye, and the furniture, though casually arranged, is mainly traditional.

The building, like the family, is expanding. The Martellas have four children between the ages of two and eight years, and the rooms in both the restaurant and the apartment constantly change use according to their needs. "The Room," a new addition on the main floor, is used for courses in language and linguini conducted by Roberto, but its long wooden table is also where the children have dinner after school and do their homework, watched over by

The kitchen stands at the heart of this family's life.

Dressed for Easter Sunday, two of the children pose for the camera.

Lucia prepares a spezzatino *for Easter Sunday lunch.*

Carrying the food downstairs.

A side table laden with delicacies.

OVERLEAF: *Specially prepared dishes are laid out on the table next to the kitchen before being carried downstairs for lunch.*

Three generations at the table.

The master bedroom.

Lucia. The large television set suspended amid the hanging basketware is used not only to watch world soccer matches but also to show Italian films or as a visual aid in language classes.

"The Room" is also used to entertain a myriad family relations. As many as thirty may sit down to lunch on Easter Sunday. The feast begins at noon and continues all day, each course prepared upstairs by Lucia with the help of her mother, then carried down to the Room. The menu consists mainly of food from Puglia, the region in Italy where Lucia's parents came from. Lamb is a traditional Easter dish, either marinated and roasted with herbs and served with fried potatoes and fresh green beans, or baked slowly in the oven with escarole and ricotta cheese. The pasta, *cavatappi al*

coniglio, is, of course, like everything else, home-made.

The hopes and ambitions of this extraordinary couple are expressed through their vision for Grano. They see it as more than just a place to eat; it is also an Italian cultural experience. Language lessons, poetry readings and musical evenings are only the beginning — they also have plans for a cooking school and art gallery upstairs.

Living as they do on Yonge Street, Toronto's main north-south artery, the city is their backyard. "People around us in the shops and the people who live above the shops know our children," says Roberto. "There is a real sense of community and as a family we take advantage of that." So, happily, do their customers.

29

At Home With William Perehudoff and Dorothy Knowles

A family romp in one of the canola fields on their farm.

OVERLEAF: Wearing kneepads, Bill always works on the floor in his studio.

THE HOME OF WILLIAM PEREHUDOFF, the "Farmer Painter," is situated on a bluff overlooking the Saskatchewan River, which gently winds its way through the golden fields of the Prairies. In this unique setting Bill, together with his wife, Dorothy Knowles, the well-known landscape painter, have created an artists' compound where they have raised their family and worked together for more than forty years. Each building, although newly built, reflects the vernacular origins of the property.

The land was settled in 1898 by William's Doukhobor grandfather, who came here from Bodanovka, a village in Georgia, then a part of Russia. William's internationally renowned work finds its deep roots not only in the traditions of his forefathers' love of the land but in the regional culture of Saskatoon, where the early ambitions of the young Doukhobor were nurtured by the local arts community.

Bill left school at the age of fifteen in order to help his parents on the farm, but continued to educate himself at the home of the local nurse, who was the only source of newspapers and books in the community. Given that he did not speak English until the age of ten, this was no mean achievement.

Eventually Bill decided to go abroad to seek out the work of contemporary American and European painters, and it was on his first trip to Europe in 1951 that he met the young Dorothy Knowles, who was studying at an art school in London. He persuaded her to join him in Europe and they mar-

*Unlike Bill's studio, Dorothy's
commands a sweeping view of
the Saskatchewan River.*

A prophetic picture.

A family that paints together.

ried in Paris later that year. They pooled their meager resources to study art, travelling by bus and third-class train for several months in France and Italy, where they sought out the frescoes of Giotto and Piero della Francesca.

On their voyage home to Canada by ship, they encountered a violent storm. In order to divert his attention and Dorothy's from the inevitable sea-sickness, Bill occupied himself by painting a scene of the two of them, accompanied by three little girls, marooned in a small craft tossed by the waves. The charming picture, reminiscent of a Russian icon, proved prophetic. Their first daughter Rebecca was born in 1952, followed closely by Catherine and then Carol.

The Perehudoffs' passion for painting has not escaped the second generation. Although the girls were not unduly influenced by their parents to paint, each one, in her own time, has discovered a deeply rooted desire to express herself on canvas.

They are also interested in their Doukhobor roots. Cathy's current project is a video documentary called "Write It on the Heart," which will be shown at various art galleries together with an exhibition of portraits of five contemporary Doukhobor women of different generations. Their stories will tell of how their culture, faith and belief in pacifism have affected their lives, and the exhibit will coincide with the one hundredth anniversary of the laying down and burning of government-issued guns in Russia by the Doukhobors.

This family has been rooted in the land for generations now. Bill's grandfather loved and worked the land to provide shelter and sustenance for the family, and now the younger generation find themselves returning to it to provide sustenance for the soul and inspiration for their artistic life.

AT HOME WITH ANNIE AND PIERRE CANTIN

Rooster and hens strut across the lawn behind the Manoir.

A view of the diamond-point armoire, *the couple's first major purchase.*

OVERLEAF: *Annie and Pierre and Benjy.*

THE CANTINS HAVE LIVED IN the Manoir of Charleville for thirty years. Built in the early seventeenth century it was about to be torn down when one day Pierre noticed it as he drove by. The man who owned it had had a heart attack recently and wanted to get rid of the house. Pierre went to see him in hospital and bought it. Over a period of thirty years, Annie and Pierre have replaced the roof, insulated it, installed new windows in the same style as the old, and replaced flooring, but they have preserved everything they could; the floors in the attic, for instance, are original.

In the beginning, the house, which was declared a historic site in 1965, was a weekend retreat from Montreal. Then, in 1976, the couple moved in full-time, and now they live there surrounded by their collections and a menagerie that includes a rooster named Caruso, assorted hens and ducks, and a dog, Benjy.

They began collecting old Quebec pine furniture in 1963 after they read Jean Palardy's book *Les meubles anciens du Canada français.* A large diamond-point *armoire* was their first major purchase, but they had always loved old things. Both of them came from families of collectors; Annie's parents specialized in furniture and musical boxes, while Pierre's mother collected toys, old photographs and family memorabilia and stored everything in a warehouse. Annie adds to her own collection each time she visits France, where she was born and raised.

The Cantins are indefatigable collectors. They share the

The attic is filled with
treasures.

Three of Annie's favourite
porcelain-faced dolls.

The Cantins sleep
at one end of the attic.

same tastes and are equally passionate about collecting, and have given up trips and other luxuries to indulge their obsession. They have acquired about five hundred dolls, doll carriages by the score, and almost fifty sleighs, not to mention doll houses, doll clothes and accessories, electric trains, music boxes, toy cars and toy banks — in all, more than four thousand toys. They also have old Quebec chalices, as well as costumes from the theatre, hats and bonnets from the eighteenth century, dresses of the nineteenth century, and eighteenth-century *habitant* woven linen shirts, early nineteenth-century wolfskin coats with *ceintures fléchées*, men's canes, tobacco pouches, pipes, buttons, hooked rugs and woven pieces of cloth from all over Quebec, and one thousand Christmas decorations from the nineteenth and early twentieth century.

The Cantins' treasures have come from some unusual sources. On one occasion, Annie noticed several very pretty boxes which had been put out in the garbage by a neighbour. When Annie expressed an interest in them, the neighbour asked for fifteen dollars — which Annie, of course,

paid. Another time, they bought three bags of hats from a modiste in Montreal, and Annie happily spent the whole night trying them on. The Cantins have also found extraordinary things — from paintings to reliquaries — at church bazaars in Montreal and Quebec City. They remember where they purchased everything, though they have only just started making an inventory.

Pierre is a retired architect who worked on buildings all over Quebec. Curiously, although he loves living in a very old house, his own work — in hospitals, schools, churches, arenas and other public buildings — is very contemporary in feeling. Annie, with her experience in research and design, gives expert evaluations for museums and insurance companies on old toys, dolls, furniture and costumes, the things she herself collects and loves. "We are almost prisoners of our collections," she says.

A corner of the kitchen.

A grouping of eighteenth-century habitant artifacts.

43

AT HOME WITH SUSAN AND RICHARD PERREN

Richard and Susan relaxing on the porch outside the master bedroom.

Henry windsurfing.

Brunch on the rocks.

OVERLEAF: *The living room commands a spectacular view of the water.*

AS A SMALL CHILD SUSAN PERREN spent summer holidays in the north-west of Scotland. She remembers isolation, a wild beauty of lochs and surrounding bens, and of course the sea, to which she would walk every day to play in the tidal pools. She also remembers the joy of being out in a rowboat and the boat being nudged by a whale. "A terrible excitement for a small child in a small boat."

Later childhood and adolescent summers were spent in Canada in Riding National Park in Manitoba and on Big Rideau Lake south of Ottawa, both beautiful in their way, but bland compared to the limitless horizon that the sea presented. Susan, eventually settled in Toronto, but she was lucky enough to be invited to a friend's island in Georgian Bay — la mer douce. "I was enchanted by this island paradise set in a shining sea and I have remained enchanted."

With her husband-to-be, gemmologist Richard Perren, she went back to Georgian Bay to stay with Richard's grand-

father at Point au Baril. The accommodation was simple, but that was not important — fishing was. "Morning and afternoon we set out in Grampy's boat *The Sea Q* with Mike, Grampy's Indian guide, at the helm. He took them to his spots — places with names like Bread Basket Kish Kadena — where they always caught fish, which was later cooked by Mike on the rocks of an outer island."

As a married couple, Susan and Richard continued to spend a part of every summer in Georgian Bay, renting cottages on various islands including Windward, which has been their summer retreat for the past six years. Windward is a small patch of land on the edge of a very large island which consists of thousands of acres of Crown land. In the midst of a wilderness of small lakes and the habitat of bear, deer, beaver and blue heron, the Perrens look onto a bay and beyond that to an endless horizon of open water. An island in the bay protects them from the worst of Georgian Bay's blow, but they can still see and hear it at its wildest.

Their existence at Windward is unplanned. Susan says, "We get up at dawn sometimes and go out in the canoe for an hour or so — it is still then — or I read all night and go to sleep at dawn."

For the Perrens, Windward allows an opportunity to think or do nothing. Everyone in the family loves the place for his or her own reasons. For Richard, "It is a completely stripped-down life. No frills. A day may be spent reading, swimming, sailing, anticipating the excitement of a storm, reading the sky to check the weather by the way the sun goes down in the evening. There are no rules. It has a peacefulness that allows one to think in a different way."

Susan talks of the pink moccasin flowers in the spring, the delicate purple iris sibirica that find a toehold in a rock and bloom in Japanese-like arrangements; the terror and fascination of coming upon sleeping fox snakes and occasionally a very wakeful rattlesnake; exploring the

A classic Canadian cottage kitchen.

A simple but comfortable guest cabin.

OVERLEAF: *The interior of the guest cabin.*

back bays and seeking out needle-nose garfish, masses of them in the back bays.

Max, their older son, spends his time birdwatching. Young Henry will watch for the wind to pick up, and disappear only to be sighted again whizzing across the bay on his windsurfer.

For Richard, Windward "is our children's home. It is what Canada is about. The igneous rock scraped bare by glacier activity. The opportunistic growth of shallow-rooted pine trees. The severity in Georgian Bay allows one to explore one's interior landscape."

Susan says, "A number of years ago, I had an encounter with a bear. I was wakened one morning about 6:30 by a sort of a bump on the cottage wall. I got out of bed and walked into the kitchen and there I found myself nose to nose, a screen separating us, with a large black bear with a grizzled snout. Oh the terror! Oh the excitement! I was transfixed. It took its time to lope off to its summer territory in the wilderness. It was as though the landlord had come to see how the tenants were doing. Was this the adult counterpart to my childhood encounter with the whale bumping against the boat?"

Max and Henry go canoeing at
the end of the day.

AT
HOME
WITH

CHIEF
CY
STANDING
AND
AVA
HILL

Ava's collection of baskets from around the world.

A vitrine crowded with fine examples of Native crafts.

A favourite family lunch.

CHIEF CY STANDING AND AVA HILL live in a small wooden house at the end of a narrow dusty road on the Wahpeton Dakota Reserve near Prince Albert, Saskatchewan.

On entering the house, one is struck first by a large collection of woven baskets made by indigenous peoples all over the world. Looking around, one begins to realize that Ava is a born collector. The walls of the family room in her basement, for instance, are covered with posters, old and new, of Native conferences held across North America. Buttons collected from various Native pow-wows are also on display, and the furniture is draped with Indian star blankets. Hand-crafted snowshoes, beaded moccasins and an exquisite buffalo-hide coat are hung on the walls as artifacts to be handled and admired. Ava also collects quill-work pictures and Native dolls from around the world.

Ava is a Mohawk from the Six Nations tribe of the Grand River Reserve near Brantford, Ontario. Active in Native affairs since the age of seventeen, she has devoted many years to the cause of her people, having worked both at the Chiefs of Ontario office in Toronto and the Assembly of First Nations in Ottawa. Before moving to Saskatchewan in 1991, she was senior executive assistant to George Erasmus, national chief of the Assembly of First Nations. But since then, she has been a homemaker, as she describes herself, for her daughter, Julie, and Cy.

Cooking traditional food is one of her many interests, and Cy comes home every day for lunch, the main meal of the day. A favourite meal might be buffalo stew, bannock and corn soup, which is made from salt pork and wild corn.

Ava's appreciation of Native crafts has led her to encourage other women on the reserve to observe old traditions and produce fine buffalo-skin moccasins and beadwork to be sold at seasonal pow-wows. She herself has begun to design and make beaded earrings, and she and Julie create

Julie's costumes for the dance competitions that take place at pow-wows.

The Wahpeton, or Leaf Dwellers, are a part of the once great Sioux nation. This band now consists of fifty families that form a community of 230 people. Since the death of the last hereditary chief of the Wahpeton Dakota nation in 1936, the elders have elected the chief from among themselves, for four-year terms.

Cy Standing, a former electronics technician for the Royal Canadian Air Force stationed in Quebec, Ontario and France, is in the middle of his third term as chief of the Wahpeton Dakota nation. In an effort to encourage his people to be more self-sufficient, a herd of bison has been established on the reserve. But Cy is also concerned with the spiritual life of his people. When he was a boy, the prevailing government policy was the integration and assimilation of Native peoples. "Today it is considered necessary to edu-

Ava works at her beading in the
basement poster room.

cate our people to understand their traditions, and to develop a knowledge of our history and to be proud of it," Cy says. "If we feel dignified by our history we are also in a position to respect other cultures and traditions." The new school on the Wahpeton Dakota Reserve is conducting Dakota language classes, and as chairman of the board of the Waneskewin Museum and Heritage Park, Cy is making sure that there is an authentic understanding of the cultural legacy of the Northern Plains Indians. The return to the use of the sweat lodge, which is a symbol of spiritual cleansing, is another important development in the renewal of Native traditions.

Working together, Cy and Ava seem to have realized their dream:

> May the warm winds of Heaven blow softly on this house and may the Great Spirit bless all who live here.

Julie practising for a pow-wow.

Cy in his ceremonial chief's headdress.

Checking on the bison which roam freely over the Dakota lands.

The sweat lodge.

57

Eight hours a day, six days
a week, Mordecai writes.

At
Home
With

Mordecai
and
Florence
Richler

"THIS IS HOME TO ME, YES. We have had several homes, but we bought this in 1975 and have lived here longer than anywhere. I can work better out here. We go into town once a week, have lunch, see friends and our son Jake, buy food and come home."

Mordecai Richler is one of Canada's pre-eminent writers, and for twenty years he has lived in a house high on a hill overlooking Lake Memphremagog with his wife, Florence, mother of five children, Mordecai's muse, his champion and manager of their daily lives.

Seated in her sitting room, a small, comfortable, intimate space lined with shelves full of books on gardening and gardens, Florence talks easily about her family. "We have five children: Daniel has published a novel and is working on a new book, Emma is an actress, Noah a radio producer for the BBC and a writer, Martha an art historian, and Jake writes for the Mirror in Montreal and is thinking of going to law school." The children live in England, the United States and other parts of Canada, but they still come home to be together in the house by the lake at Christmas time.

Florence seems perfectly content and serene. "It is a privileged life here. I have my books, the garden, music, and I cook." Since her husband works at home all day, she says "We spend an awful lot of time together; we have always done it, even in very small quarters. In the first flat we had, Mordecai's desk had to be covered in the evening to set up the drinks tray — every room had a dual purpose. Mordecai can't bear noise when he works, so our children were taught at a very early age to walk about on tiptoes in bare feet. It was only after they had visited other people's houses that they learnt that not everybody spoke in whispers. Needless to say, they were not left with any romantic ideas about writing." When the children are at home, they know they can't sit and talk on the terrace below Mordecai's writing room on the second floor until his work day is done, which is the reason Florence extended the kitchen and built a conservatory and back porch as a retreat for the noisy.

A few years ago Florence built Mordecai a snooker room because he had fond memories of playing the game as a boy. Now, every Boxing Day, there is a snooker tournament for

the Richler Cup. It starts around 11:00 a.m., with a lunch break for chili con carne. Acquaintances from the local pub, the children and their friends all compete.

The house is filled with books; walls in all living spaces except the snooker room are lined with floor-to-ceiling bookcases. Mordecai's writing room, with a sweeping vista of the lake, is no exception.

Highly disciplined, he works six days a week, starting very early in the morning, breaking for lunch and a rest, then putting in another two hours in the afternoon. "I concen-trate on one book for four or five months at a time, then do something else for a month — go on a trip, do something else to get away from it. I have always worked at home, usu-ally go to the local pub around four. Deadlines are not im-portant — I'm already three years late on my next novel." Mordecai now writes on an electric typewriter as it was getting too difficult to get parts for his manual typewriter; computers are not part of his writing idiom. "I love to write, I really enjoy it. It is a much easier life than most people lead."

Florence built the snooker room to fulfil a boyhood dream of Mordecai's.

Florence cutting herbs on the porch outside the kitchen.

At Home With Brian and Marilyn MacKay-Lyons

ON A SUNLIT DECK OUTSIDE THEIR HOME in Halifax, two little girls sit painting their toenails the same cherry-red colour as the fire ladders their father incorporates into his work as an architect. Their home, a converted gas station in the heart of the city, is a perfect example of the way in which Brian MacKay-Lyons appropriates existing motifs and makes them his own.

The home he has created here is open and inviting. It includes both work and living spaces. His office is on the ground floor, and there's a conference room on the second; the rest is private, but it fronts on both the street and the second-floor deck.

The family's rural retreat is also a mix of new and old. Brian bought it shortly after he and his wife, Marilyn, returned to Nova Scotia from California. He had spent the previous four years completing a graduate program at UCLA under the tutelage of Charles Moore who, together with Robert Venturi, was the founder of the post-modernist movement in architecture.

Marilyn and Brian were first attracted to this pure white Cape Cod house because of its view of the ocean, the composition of the group of buildings and the surrounding fields and valleys. The main house originally had thirteen tiny rooms. Brian set about gutting the interior and Marilyn

This converted gas station fronts on three streets in Halifax.

*The recreation area is flanked
by a conference room on the left,
bedrooms on the right.*

*The main living space and
kitchen: one of Brian's favourite
motifs is the traditional Acadian
red fire ladder.*

The downstairs office.

64

describes it in this way, "He went at it with a crowbar with no idea of how it might develop." He would say to Marilyn, "Lie down here, this would be a good place for a bedroom." So there she would test out the spot among the rubble.

The house began life 240 years ago as a cabin made of logs insulated with seaweed and wrapped in birchbark. The clapboard exterior was added later, in the 1800s. Marilyn describes it as a crooked little house, so for Brian the first challenge was to make it plumb. It was in fact two feet off the vertical. He achieved balance by building a house within a house. As a result the windows became very deep as they spanned the layering of time. A tapering tower was erected slightly off-centre — it houses a stone fireplace, a bathroom and sleeping places and closets.

At one point in the building process, when Brian decided to use red ladders instead of a staircase to link the central structure, Marilyn began to think he was crazy.

The house was not planned for children, but as it turns out it is a child's paradise. The red ladders are used to climb to the sleeping loft and the openings in the mezzanine wall allow the children to peer through and keep a watchful eye on their parents below.

The MacKay-Lyons' country retreat in Kingsburg, Nova Scotia.

*The interior was gutted
and rebuilt from scratch.*

*A summer feast of lobster
is eaten on the beach.*

*Brian enjoys drumming
after dinner.*

Brian and Marilyn are a rarity in our place and time: theirs is an arranged marriage; their fathers met at a furniture convention and decided that a match should be made between the two. The couple were introduced some time later, when Marilyn was seventeen, and they have been together ever since. They tease nine-year-old daughter Renee that she has only eight years left.

AT
HOME
WITH

JACK
AND
LILY
PEMBERTON

*Jack checks a carriage
before a drive.*

A GLEAMING COACH IS PULLED by perfectly turned-out matched pairs of horses, bright-eyed with manes and tails flying, tack brilliant from hours of hand-rubbing with saddle soap. Keeping this moving equipage safely on the road requires courage, experience and technical craft. Jack Pemberton illustrates this when he recalls the time he was out in a field on his Ontario farm, training with a carriage and four around a slalom course of barrels. The lead horse knocked over a forty-gallon steel drum, and as the drum rolled underneath the carriage, it went under the front axle, lifting the carriage in the air. Jack was thrown off the seat upside down, still holding on to the reins, his head between the galloping hooves and the turning wheels.

Jack has acquired some 150 carriages over a span of forty years. Lily, his wife, is very patient and understanding but has absolutely no interest in horses or carriages.

"I had a jumper before I got married and I tried to hitch it to a sleigh which I had bought and restored, thinking I could take Lily for a ride. I realized that I liked fixing carriages up and so I started buying them — and all of a sudden I had ten of them. I then bought a pair of horses and learned how to drive."

Jack learned how to drive on local roads and farms. He mastered the finer points of driving by associating with fellow enthusiasts in the U.S. and the U.K. The Carriage Association of America was formed in 1962; Jack became its president in 1967.

He had started competing at local fall fairs in the early sixties. At that time he was the only one in his area to pleasure-drive, and he won his first big four-in-hand class at the Royal Winter Fair by default. Driving against Bud McDougall and one other competitor he got lucky. McDougall's professional driver went off course and the remaining competitor had had too rich a meal and knocked over all the obstacles. In the days when Jack showed a lot, he and Lily, Morris Kerr, his professional horseman, and

his wife and a groom would take a Park Drag and a Roof Seat Brake and five horses, one being a "spare," to big shows in Pennsylvania, Virginia and South Carolina. He was then the only Canadian in both American and British coaching associations. Today in Southern Ontario alone there are three pleasure-driving organizations with regular turnouts of as many as a hundred coaches.

Jack likes to drive, but he loves carriages. "I am a buggy nut, I don't pretend to be a horseman. I enjoy turning out my carriages, I try to achieve perfection. The details in very many small things are important — the colour of the lap robe against the upholstery, for instance, or you can't have brass buttons on the livery with silver on the harness." Jack's favourite carriages are a bird's eye-maple Bronson wagon once owned by the Sifton family and a Park Drag originally used to attend sporting events like the hunt or the races.

Besides the carriages, he has one hundred sides of harnesses, sixty pairs of carriage lamps, twenty sets of livery which include postilion livery, livery used for royalty and livery especially suited to certain carriages. Each set includes hats, boots, coats, vests and gloves.

Jack's collections are stored and maintained on a small farm in Southern Ontario run by his daughter Ellen and her husband, Juan. One very devoted woman helps clean,

Cleaning livery and harnesses is full-time work.

Some of the 150 carriages in Jack's collection.

A summer picnic.

polish, brush, dust and vacuum all these treasured objects. The tack and harnesses are rubbed with a special wax every three months, whether they have been used or not, in order to maintain their suppleness. Carriage wheels are turned every six months so that they will not flatten. Mothballs and pepper are scattered on the upholstery to keep away the moths and mice.

"I am not known for liking life in the fast lane, I prefer the slow lane, and going for a quiet drive is like turning back the clock." In recognition of Jack's pre-eminence in the world of coaching, he spends most of his time now judging combined driving in the U.S., England, Germany, Austria, Holland and Belgium.

Going on a drive with Jack, the wind and sun on one's face, it's easy to see the appeal of life in the slow lane.

AT
HOME
WITH

*Colin consults with a
model in the living space.*

*A fashion shoot in the
studio area.*

COLIN
FAULKNER

WHEN FASHION PHOTOGRAPHER Colin Faulkner moved into
an industrial building in Toronto three years ago, the space
was completely empty. The landlord erected interior walls
to Colin's specifications.

Grand double doors, seen from the studio space looking towards the living area, open onto a storage room.

A table is wheeled into the studio for a meal.

Originally, one large space doubled as work and living area, but Colin recently took over the adjoining apartment, creating an L-shaped corner flat. One arm is a studio, with an office, darkroom, kitchen and bathroom tucked in; the other is living space.

Although the impression is one of comfort, everything is meticulously placed — boxes arranged in rows, paintings stacked against one wall. The dinner-table, which is on wheels — literally a moveable feast — is moved into the studio area for parties.

Born in Nova Scotia, Colin spent the first seven years of his life in Thailand, where his father was director of the Bangkok YMCA. He grew up in London, Ontario, and attended Fanshawe College, a school he describes as "highly technical" in training. After working for several years as an assistant to other photographers, he went out on his own.

Colin is a collector — of wood, metal and anything else he finds on front lawns. The results range from home-made wooden cabinets to what Colin calls "assemblages" — sculptures created from the objects he finds. They aren't static: if Colin finds something new, he'll change the configuration.

Colin's home is an elegant, austere space, but nonetheless welcoming.

Found objects are carefully arranged in what Colin calls "assemblages."

The storage room is crammed with things.

80

AT HOME WITH VALERIE AND JOHN LAXTON

It took two days to arrange the flowers.

WHEN VALERIE AND JOHN LAXTON ran off and got married in a registry office in England after the war, neither had any money, so they used Valerie's savings of eleven pounds to buy the wedding ring. In the spring of 1957, they arrived in Montreal, then travelled across the country in a beat-up station wagon, reaching Vancouver on Thanksgiving weekend. Sitting on a point of land looking out at Garrow Bay, they decided that this was the most beautiful place on earth, and seven years later they moved into the house they now live in.

When their daughter Chandra was to be married, she was determined to fulfil a childhood wish to hold the ceremony "at the beach" — a strip of land stretching from a breakwater at the bottom of a cliff.

This required much preparation, and Valerie began in January to make arrangements for the August wedding. She quickly got in touch with caterer Peter Weiser, whom she had met when he had come to the house as Sean Connery's personal chef during the filming of a commercial. Over the next few months, he and Valerie planned the menu together — fish, flesh, fowl and vegetables, which translated into a

savoury ragout of scallops, shrimp, lobster tails and salmon in a Chablis sauce; tournedos with sauce chausseur; sesame and lemon chicken; and a stir-fry with tofu. A light chocolate wedding cake was chosen after many weeks of sampling at Sunday-night dinners.

Marriages may be made in heaven, but in every complex, live performance there are hitches, the unforeseen that threatens pandemonium. One such problem was the wedding dress. Says Chandra, "Mum and I went down to Seattle, and a designer from San Francisco fitted the dress I had chosen. Four months later, I picked it up off the bus in Bellingham, left it hanging in the cupboard for a few days and finally a week before the wedding, tried it on." To her horror, the dress was too small, and it had French seams — a nightmare to alter. Fortunately, a local seamstress was able to remake the bodice completely.

Then, the day before the wedding, just when preparations were at their peak, there was a breakdown of the Laxton Pacific railway, the inclined elevator on the cliff that would carry the food, liquor, flowers and catering staff. To everyone's great relief, the elevator was fixed in time, and the

Unpacking bouquets.

Final touches to the dinner-tables in the tent.

Valerie Laxton arrives by
funicular from the house above.

The father and the bride.

Chandra and Horst at the altar.

florists were able to finish decorating the wedding arbour and the tent with fuchsia, purple and white lilies, roses, daisies and chrysanthemums.

Valerie faced a dilemma when she was unable to decide which dress to wear — an ivory one or a red one. Valerie's mother thought the red dress inappropriate as she did not want her granddaughter to be outdone, but Chandra advised her mother to wear the red, because, as she said, "You look so good in it."

On her wedding day, to the music of Wagner's *Lohengrin* bridal chorus, Chandra appeared with her bridesmaids at the foot of the cliff, and she and her father proceeded along the "beach" to the altar at the end of the breakwater. The scene of green grass, ocean, flowers and happiness was magical.

"The whole thing was so much better than I ever dreamed," says Chandra.

Valerie's finishing words in her toast to the bride were, "I would like everybody to raise their glass in a toast to Chandra, our daughter, the bride, for tonight again she outshines the stars." The name Chandra means moonlight.

On recollection months later, Chandra feels that she had a perfect wedding; she would not have changed a thing.

Wedding guests assemble after the ceremony.

At Home With Sonny Rainville

Sonny ties his own salmon flies and displays them in his bedroom.

The guides in the rod room checking the tackle before a morning's fishing.

SONNY RAINVILLE STANDS waist-deep in water, effortlessly throwing his line seventy-five feet out over the Grand Cascapedia River, his fly dipping to touch the water first. He has been salmon fishing here for more than sixty years. From the age of eight, when he came to stay in the area with his grandmother, and all through the 1930s right up until he went off to war in 1940, he would spend one week of every summer fishing with his father, Gus, on the Cascapedia River. In 1945, when he was discharged from bomber command, his father asked him what he most wanted to do. He said he wanted to salmon fish, and he has done so every summer since. Now retired from the investment business, Sonny bought New Derreen, his present salmon camp, in 1986, and he spends six months a year there.

The Grand Cascapedia River was originally reserved for the pleasure of the British Royal Family. Queen Victoria's daughter Princess Louise spent many a happy summer fishing here, and in 1884 the Marquis of Lansdowne, governor general of Canada, built New Derreen Camp. In 1893, when Lansdowne was made viceroy of India, New Derreen was sold to some Americans who turned it into the Cascapedia Club.

Sonny cherishes New Derreen, which was built with a Victorian sense of space and comfort. There are fireplaces in most of the rooms to keep the river damp at bay, big

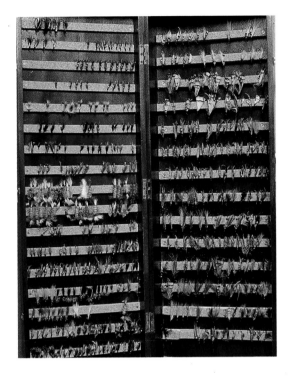 

comfortable sofas in the panelled living room and a huge old-fashioned sun porch which Sonny has filled with mementos of his fishing and hunting life.

He opens the camp in late spring, and the season starts the first week of June. It takes six fishing guides, a "shore boy," the cook and the maid two weeks of cleaning and repairing to get everything up and going and ready for Sonny's yearly gathering of guests who fill New Derreen's seven bedrooms all summer long.

Sonny's son, David, who started throwing a line when he was seven, says that on the river "you are fishing a wily competitor who wins as often as you do." If you average one salmon a day, that is very good fishing indeed, and it is most unusual to fish for a week and leave empty-handed.

Salmon fishing is more than a rod and a reel, it is a way of life, with its own language and rhythm which vary only slightly from camp to camp. You talk about pools, and each pool on the river has a name — Charlie Valley Rock, Caribou Crossing, Upper Murdock, Scow Channel — along with a history and a reputation. You "kill" your fish rather than catch it, and you throw a John Olin, a Green Highlander, a Lady Amhurst or a Bomber. Each river in the area has its own characteristic flies, depending on the colour of the water and the time of year.

At New Derreen, one day follows another in much the same pattern: breakfast is eaten any time between 6:45 and 8:00 a.m. Then Sonny and his guests are driven to their respective pools around 8:30 for the morning's sport. The guides help each guest spot the fish, pole the canoe, give advice and encouragement and net the salmon. Everyone returns to the camp for lunch and a nap, then back to the river again around 4:00 to fish until dark. At the end of the fishing day, Terry, the head guide, and his men weigh and clean any fish killed, check and dry the lines, hang up the waders and put away the fishing bags. Larry, who has worked at the camp for eleven years, takes some of the catch off to the smoke-house for smoking, a process that takes almost a week.

Sonny and his friends change for dinner. Drinks and the evening meal are usually served after the sun has set, which in the summer can be as late as 10:00 p.m.

Shirley, the cook, and Judy, her assistant, serve deliciously fattening meals — hors-d'oeuvre of smoked salmon and pâté, home-made bread, steaming casseroles, soufflés and roasts, as well as rich desserts.

After dinner, the lucky fishermen write up their catches in a logbook, including details of the pool, the fly used and the prevailing weather and water conditions. Satiated with delectable food and drink, and fish stories of the day, everyone retires to bed, to be lulled to sleep by the sound of the river.

Throwing a line on the Grand Cascapedia.

A twenty-four-pound catch.

90

Preparing the fish for the brine before smoking.

Making a salmon mousse for the evening hors-d'oeuvre.

Cotton lies in front of a fire in the living room, which is panelled in old pine.

A welcome martini at the end of the day.

A framed history of the one that didn't get away.

At

Home

With

PATRICK AMIOT AND BRIGITTE LAURENT have created a home that is whimsical, fun and perhaps a little mad. His ebullience, her tranquillity and their combined energies help meet the demands of their work as artists and the needs of their two little girls, Matilde and Ursule.

Born dyslexic, Patrick hated school and took refuge in sculpting clay. When he met Brigitte in 1981, she was about to enrol in law school, but she decided to abandon her studies and moved to Vancouver with him. There Patrick found

PATRICK

AMIOT

AND

BRIGITTE

LAURENT

Matilde wearing her favourite
tutu at the top of the stairs
leading to the living quarters.

work as a baker and Brigitte as a butcher. They rented a studio and he began making small ceramic sculptures and selling them at local craft shows. To help him, Brigitte, who had never held a paintbrush before, started painting parts of his sculptures. Finally, gambling everything, they used all their savings to rent a gallery for a week. They sold out within three hours on opening night, and their careers were launched.

After two major commissions for Expo '86, Patrick achieved local fame, and for the first time he and Brigitte had money in their pockets. A month after Expo closed, they left for the East. "Leaving Vancouver as God," says Patrick, "it was a shock to arrive in Toronto an unknown, forced to sleep in a truck for three months until we could afford a place to live." They eventually returned to Montreal because Brigitte was pregnant and wanted a house, and Montreal was affordable.

In the house they bought on De Bullion Street, there are two studios on the main floor, one in which Brigitte paints

*Patrick in the kitchen
making his special omelette,
the "Homme laid."*

*Patrick and Brigitte work
side by side in the ground-
floor studio.*

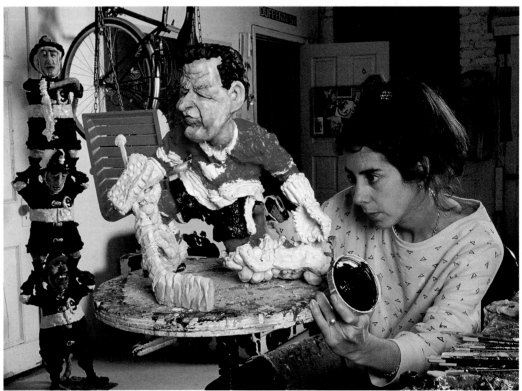

and a bigger one in which Patrick sculpts. They live upstairs in a child-centred, comfortable, eclectic space on top of which is a roof garden.

The neighbourhood is full of artists, a community of like-minded people who share ideas and trade in each other's work. Often when Patrick has finished a piece he is particularly happy about, he opens the street door of his studio and invites whoever is passing by to come in and have a look.

"After ten years away, I went from a Quebecois complex to a proud multicultural Canadian. It was difficult to settle back in Quebec, but the birth of Matilde changed my life. It built a relationship with this neighbourhood and this city because of the story of the garage door." When Brigitte was six months pregnant with Matilde, Patrick wrote on their

underwear. There is no pressure here whatsoever. In the summertime, when the doors of the studio are open, the weirdos and the rubbies on the corner are a part of me. I'm building my family in this house. I've finally come home."

garage door in large letters, "*On va avoir un bébé*," and he added different messages about the imminent birth every few days right up until Matilde was born. Neighbours, the local press, firemen and the police kept track of the messages and dropped off good wishes and presents. Matilde became known as the "De Bullion Baby" and the experience took Patrick and Brigitte back to their roots in Quebec.

People drop in often because they know that both Patrick and Brigitte are likely to be at home. "Brigitte usually does the cooking and I do the entertaining. I like to talk, she doesn't. We don't go out much, we have a house. Most of our friends don't, so they come here."

In addition to sculpting, Patrick has made furniture, such as the "spoon highchair" for Matilde and the light fixtures in the upstairs apartment. He would like to make all his furniture, finish the roof garden, create a custom car. "Sculpting is almost too much like work; making toys and things for the children is more fun. For so long I was so ambitious. Right now I just want to have my kids around."

Asked why he loves his house, Patrick replies, "I can be who I am. I can get the milk at the corner in my long

Dressed up for a family portrait.

The "spoon highchair" and the swing are just two of the objects Patrick has created to amuse his children.

OVERLEAF: Patrick's sense of fun is evident even in the design of the bathroom.

At Home With James Coutts

Jim carefully plans and seeds his poppy garden every year.

A walk through caragana hedges planted by Jim's grandfather in 1918.

THE DEFINITION OF A HOMESTEAD in Canadian terms could be a small wooden house built on a quarter-section in the Prairies. In an effort to encourage settlement, land was often given to people — on the condition that they build a house within two years. James Coutts's grandfather William Allan, who came to the Prairies in 1903, was one of those who took advantage of the offer.

Bill had only been in Nanton, Alberta a short while when the homesteading bug hit him. In order to stay with the railway, where he was an agent, farm and proceed with his plans to marry and settle he needed help, and so he sent for his father and brother to take up land close by.

In the uncompromising landscape of the Prairies, Bill built a small house for his new wife, Mabel, and baby daughter, Alberta. His love affair with the railway meant that he spent a lot of time away from home, and it is a tribute to his wife that she bore four young children at the homestead and raised them virtually alone. But the family later sold the place and moved into the town of Nanton, where Bill established himself as a carpenter.

In 1980, much to the chagrin of his mother, Alberta, James Coutts decided to try to buy back his grandfather's farm. "What do you want that old place for?" she asked. James persisted and was successful, and today, within an hour's drive of Calgary, you will find a neatly arranged wooden house set in a very pretty garden overlooking fields and, in the distance, the Porcupine Hills.

On arrival to spend the weekend at Jim's homestead, a guest will be greeted at the door by Sukhlal Patel, Jim's houseman. One may be invited to make a tour of the gardens. A walk through the poppy garden in its mid-summer splendour leads to the prairie grasses that have been cleverly planted to blend into the landscape and at the same time regenerate it for the future.

One frequent guest is Jim's mother. At the age of ninety-one, Alberta has lost none of her vim and vigour. When asked where she thinks Jim got his creative energy from, without hesitation she replies, "From me, of course. I ought to know, because I have none left!"

After a delicious dinner of chicken Stroganoff prepared by Sukhlal, a game of gin rummy is in order. Alberta challenges Jim with a "How'd you like to get beat?" And she does beat him, as well as most visitors.

Sunday may bring a picnic with a hike through the Prince of Wales Ranch, which was owned and managed by the late Duke of Windsor until 1962. An expedition to a nearby slough can lead to sightings of sandpipers, American avocets, whimbrels and plovers.

The garden is Jim's pride and joy, and he spends many hours during the winter designing how it might look in the spring. He created it from the wilderness, planting only what is native to the area or appropriate for the climatic zone. He has a strong desire to restore the Prairie meadows, and to that end he is experimenting with different grasses in his nursery. The result is a happy blend of the domestic and the wild.

Warm late afternoon light bathes the living room.

Houseman Sukhlal Patel welcomes guests upon arrival.

A guest room decorated with memorabilia of the Duke of Windsor, who once owned the neighbouring ranch.

The Coutts house, simply furnished and filled with family memorabilia, is extremely cosy. Today Alberta says that she would not have been so rude about Jim buying the place if she had known how attractive it was going to be.

Jim is a man who likes to take on challenges, whether in business or in politics. Born in Nanton some fifty years ago, he graduated from Harvard with an MBA and worked as a consultant for McKinsey and Company. He then entered the world of politics, where he became secretary to Prime Minister Lester B. Pearson and later principal secretary to Prime Minister Pierre Elliot Trudeau. He is currently chairman of Canadian Investment Capital Limited and the proud owner of the Nanton Water Company, which bottles spring water from Nanton.

But Jim doesn't want to be typecast. As he says, "I do not see myself as a businessman, any more than I'd call myself a politician or a lawyer. I guess I've always had tasks rather than jobs — something that isn't forever. I feel the same way about places: you're just passing through."

*Alberta Coutts always beats
her son at gin rummy.*

Sunday afternoon.

AT HOME WITH OLA AND FUNMI KASSIM

Morning rush: getting ready for school and office.

Lola helps Femi with her hair.

YOU DON'T GET TO SIT DOWN VERY OFTEN when you are eating your cake and having it too. Life's wicked irony in the last decade of the twentieth century is that with all our comforts and time-saving devices we seem to have less time than ever as we keep expanding our own horizons and demanding more of ourselves. Ola and Funmi Kassim deal with this paradox with energy, discipline and a strong sense of possibility. The basis for all this drive is their own family background and their devotion to their three daughters, Jumi, Lola and Femi. Long hours, long days are required to cover two medical practices, guide, chauffeur, and emotionally support the children, run a household and still have time to pursue volunteer activities in the community. However, as Funmi says, "I would like the children to have choices and some control over their lives."

Ola and Funmi met in Lagos, where they were both born. They came to Canada together in 1977 to do post-graduate work at the University of Toronto. Today, Ola, a clinical pathologist, is the director of laboratories and pathologist-in-chief at Parry Sound District General and St. Joseph's in Parry Sound, South Muskoka Memorial Hospital and Bracebridge and Huntsville Memorial Hospital. In a typical week, he begins each day by dropping Jumi off at Bishop Strachan School around 7:00 a.m., and commutes two and a half hours to Parry Sound, where he works at the first two hospitals and covers the other two when he is on call. During his long, monotonous daily drives, he listens to

professional tapes, because fifty percent of his job is administration and "I work out the problems so by the time I get to the hospital I can concentrate on the medical aspects of my job — clinical diagnosis, which is what I love best." He is also starting work on a master's degree in business administration at the University of Colorado by computer correspondence, and eventually, when the children are grown, he wants to go to law school. To relax, he listens to music — modern jazz, Nina Simone, Ella Fitzgerald, something classical — or works on the computer with the children. In the broader community, he supports the African Annual Music Awards, is a director of the Association of Nigerians in Canada, a patron of the Yoruba Cultural and Heritage

Sharing the day's events before dinner.

Each of the girls has a computer in her room.

Lola, who at one time sang with the Canadian Children's Opera Chorus, plays both the piano and the cello, and Femi, the youngest, plays the piano; they both take part in the music programs at Havergal College.

This is very much a child-centred home. As Funmi says, "The only tangible thing you can leave on earth are your children, so it is important to have a positive influence on them. Being a parent is a unique opportunity to mould something that breathes and grows on its own and becomes independent. If we can't leave the world a better place, we should try not to leave it any worse."

Association of Canada and a member of the Rotary Club of Richmond Hill.

The day starts for Funmi at 6:00 every morning and ends around midnight. A psychiatrist, she finds private practice very satisfying but would also like to teach some day. When she is at home, however, she is mummy.

"We feel at home here in Canada," she says. "It is not something I think a lot about as I tend to get on with things and we travel a lot between Nigeria, England and New York. There is a system here and the system usually does what it should — be it justice, medical or political. Our extended family in Canada are the schools the kids go to, the fishmonger at Kensington Market who has been there for over ten years, the kids' piano teacher — in other words, people who go along with the kids and fit into our life, and of course some of my colleagues, especially the female GPs. Roni's Yarn Store and bookstores are places I go to relax. The kids will always come with me to buy books." Funmi unwinds by knitting or doing needlepoint or crocheting.

The children have interests of their own — swimming, band practice, Brownies — but music is a strong common family interest. Funmi feels learning to play an instrument "is an extension of achieving discipline and learning skills through practice and concentration." She herself learnt to play the mandolin from her father and sang in the church choir. Jumi started taking piano lessons when she was three and took up the saxophone when she got to high school.

Music is an integral part of this family's life together.

In the library at the end of the day.

111

AT
HOME
WITH

ALEX
AND
RHODA
COLVILLE

AN ARTIST OF international standing, Alex Colville has always taken his inspiration from what he sees around him. He and his wife, Rhoda, have chosen to live in the small town of Wolfville, Nova Scotia, and most of his paintings portray the landscape — both natural and human — of the area.

Born in Toronto, Alex came to live in the province as a young boy when his father, who was a steel worker, was transferred. Rhoda, on the other hand, can trace her family back to farmers who settled the area in the early 1760s.

The house they live in was built in the 1920s by Rhoda's father, a prominent house-builder in the area. She was born in the house, but returned to live there with Alex only after her mother died in 1993.

The style of the building is a perfect example of 1920s four-square module and has recently been listed as a good building of the period by the Wolfville Heritage Foundation. The interior, with wooden detailing throughout, is spacious and calming. It is simply arranged with antiques and furniture made by Rhoda's father in the twenties. Many of the walls are hung with serigraphs of Colville's paintings. "They are my only record of a lifetime's work," says Colville.

For four decades Alex has used the room at the top of

the house as a studio. It is a large, spare, neatly organized space, and indeed the rest of the house also reflects a rigorously ordered, apparently serene life. And yet a closer look provides an eerie reminder of the subjects of many of Alex's sometimes disturbing paintings.

The family bathroom, austere and plainly tiled in the style of the twenties, takes on a provocative quality when one recalls the painting *Woman in a Bathtub*, which seems to suggest the terrors of a patient in an asylum. The sewing table in Rhoda's sitting room on the second floor is the table on which the revolver is placed in the menacing portrait titled *Pacific*.

Animals are part of Alex's and Rhoda's life and they appear in numerous pictures: the mongrel dog, Min, in *Stove*, for instance, and the Siamese cat, Dog, in *Cat*. Although Alex's images appear to be drawn casually from

Alex in the living room of the house in which Rhoda was born and brought up.

Rhoda at her desk in her sitting room.

Life imitates art: a photograph of Rhoda and Min inspired by Alex's painting, Stove.

OVERLEAF: The artist's regular eight-mile ride to Evangeline Beach.

daily life, they are in fact carefully planned and meticulously worked on with the precision of a master artist and draughtsman. In Alex's words a painting is "made," while a photograph is "taken." He says "The intensity of the concentration is exhausting," and he sometimes wonders if he will ever have a new idea.

Alex's daily routine may begin with an eight-mile bicycle ride to the couple's tiny cottage on Evangeline Beach. He then paints intensely for about four hours. No one is allowed to venture across the threshold of the studio until the picture in progress is completed. His output is not prolific; in eleven years he has produced only thirty-three works, or roughly three every year. It usually takes Alex almost eleven months to complete one painting — and often the gestation period before he puts brush to canvas lasts for years.

For relaxation Alex enjoys carpentry — small pieces of furniture for the house, shelves for the kitchen, a closet for Rhoda. He is also designing a small house based on Le Corbusier's principles. Occasionally, he visits his gun club for a spot of target practice.

Together he and Rhoda find great pleasure in small-town life, working, savouring the countryside around them, enjoying visits from their children and grandchildren.

Alex scrutinizing a serigraph in his third-floor studio.

On the beach.

AT HOME WITH THE CISTERCIAN MONKS OF NOTRE DAME

The heart of the monastery is the chapel, where the monks come together for seven periods of prayer each day.

LIVING HARMONIOUSLY TOGETHER in a secluded part of beautiful Hockley Valley in Southwestern Ontario is a family of nine monks, three novices, a pair of mute swans, a cockatiel and a large collie named Sybil. They all make their home in the Cistercian Monastery of Notre Dame, the only English-speaking male cloistered monastery in Canada.

For centuries monks have prayed together and lived by the labour of their own hands, seeking through the monastic life a pathway to inner strength. Cistercians are followers of the rule of St. Benedict, who founded the Trappist Order in France in the sixth century AD.

The order came into existence as a result of a desire to return to the original simplicity of the Benedictine tradition, which was being eroded by the demands of Christian society at the time. The fervour of the monks led them to the plains of Western France, where, among the wild cistus, they set up a simple monastic home and became known as the Cistercians.

The first Cistercians in Canada established themselves at Oka, Quebec in 1881. Father John Doutre entered the monastery there at the age of nineteen. Ten years ago he came to Hockley Valley.

Abbot Father John's mandate is to turn the monastery into an abbey. The number of monks required to achieve the status of an abbey is twelve, and Father John anticipates that this will take at least another ten years. "If this were Africa or the Philippines it would only take half the time. At present we have one novice remaining who will complete the six-year apostasy, out of three who felt they had a vocation. We do not recruit; it is a mutual choosing. Our message to the world outside would be that to dedicate yourself to God can be a fulfilling life — I feel real fulfilment."

Although the monks have chosen to renounce the

121

The monks produce 100,000 pounds of fruit cake each year. It is the main source of income for the monastery.

At mealtime, only readings break the strictly observed rule of silence.

Manual labour is considered a form of prayer.

temporal life, Father John says, "In a small monastery like this we are a family and have a kind of family life. We are very close."

The monks' day begins with vigils at 4:30 a.m. and at 7:30 a.m., continuing with lauds and Eucharist at 9:00 a.m. and terce and sext at 11:00 a.m. and 1:00 p.m., respectively. Between each period of prayer the monks spend their time in manual labour, attending to the needs of the monastery, cooking, cleaning, doing the laundry and maintaining the grounds and garden. After lunch and sext there is a period of prayer and spiritual reading.

Walking is the men's main relaxation. It is the only time spent alone and it is also a time for exercise. They return to chapel for vespers at 4:45 p.m., followed by dinner and compline at 8:15 p.m., then retire for the evening.

As contemplatives, all of this occurs under the strict observance of silence. The rhythm of the day and the ritual of the liturgy serve to remind one of the presence of God. The rule of St. Benedict asks the monk to leave behind the values and comforts of the world. St. Benedict believed that

a monk is to seek silence so that he can hear God's words and respond to them. He is to seek a humble life in order to be free to obey, and to obey in order to lead a divine life in harmony with the will of God.

In accordance with the monastic tradition, the monks of Notre Dame operate a guest house so that visitors may escape the clamouring of the outside world. As many as 500 people have accepted the hospitality of the monastery. "Those who come and share our prayers are our link with society. We need to be reminded that the monastery is a house of God. We are called to live in a house of God and others are called to visit it," says Father John.

The monks' main source of income is their own bakery. They produce 100,000 pounds of fruit cake, which are distributed throughout the province. The fruit cake is made from a recipe from the kitchen of one of the monks' grandmothers; it dates back to 1908. Many parishes and church organizations sell the cake as a means of fundraising.

A touching passage in a pamphlet kept at the monastery describes what the monks endeavour to achieve every day.

The contemplative, through his deeds, is striving to reflect "the burning tranquillity of his interior life. It above all is the silent witness and the unconscious testimony to the love of God, for he preaches sermons by the way he walks, the way he stands, the way he picks things up and holds them in his hands, and by the reverence with which he makes his whole life an offering of worship to God."

A woodland shrine to the Virgin Mary.

Reading and reflection are part of the daily routine.

OVERLEAF: The monks' cemetery overlooks the beautiful Hockley Valley.

AT
HOME
WITH
THE
GOVERNOR
GENERAL

Maitre d'hôtel Richard
Legrand briefing footmen
in the Ballroom.

Ironing table and bed linen
in the laundry room.

Preparing the State Bedroom.

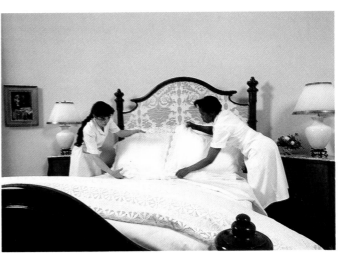

THE FOOTMEN HAD LAID THE TABLES in the Ballroom earlier in the day, the freshly laundered damask tablecloths coming directly from the laundry without a fold. Each fork and knife had been precisely positioned with the help of a ruler. A calligraphed place card and menu card were put in front of each of the one hundred guests invited to a state dinner at Rideau Hall to honour the president of the Argentine Republic. The centrepieces of late spring flowers had arrived from the Greenhouse at the last minute. In the kitchens, the head chef and sous-chef had been prepping and cooking for two days. A first course of lobster and artichokes with green beans was to be followed by sugar snap pea soup with onion confit and chicken tarragon dumpling. The main course was to be oven-roasted loin of lamb with asparagus flan, then a cheese course of St. Benoit du Lac blue cheese with Parmesan biscuit, and finally a dessert of chocolate and praline with nougatine. After a cocktail reception in the Long Gallery, each guest was announced and presented to Their Excellencies, Ramon and Gerda Hnatyshyn, and the guest of honour before preceding to the Ballroom to sit down for dinner.

In 1838 Thomas MacKay, a stonemason and early industrialist, built a two-storey stone house on thirty-five hectares of land which would slowly evolve over the next hundred and fifty years to become what is today Rideau Hall, the Canadian governor general's official residence in Ottawa. Various governors general continued to enlarge and add to the house. They also paid attention to the grounds: during the first World War, the Duke of Connaught started planting maples and other deciduous trees around the house, a tradition that is maintained today when heads of state commemorate each visit to Rideau Hall by planting a tree in the grounds.

In the course of a year, Their Excellencies host many different types of ceremonies and events: investitures for the Order of Canada, decorations for bravery and military merit, receptions for youth achievement award winners, Olympic athletes, school safety patrollers and scholarship winners, state dinners and more. The list is endless. And Rideau Hall is where the Queen and foreign heads of state stay and are entertained when they visit Ottawa.

With so many guests, the activity in the house is frenzied and the organization needed to put Canada's best foot forward is systematic and rigorous — music, invitations, food, menu cards, table settings, seating plans, ceremonial protocol for each event, speeches, even flowers are planned down to the last detail.

The Greenhouse at Rideau Hall supplies many of the flowers and plants used in the floral arrangements around the house. From it and the surrounding garden also come

Her Excellency Gerda Hnatyshyn in a planning meeting with her assistants.

The calligrapher at work on the place cards.

The Greenhouse supplies flowers and plants for all the official residences in Ottawa.

Buffing the silver.

herbs, salad vegetables and fruit in season. Everything is prepared to exacting standards that should make us feel proud of our national home, from the meticulously planned menus to the fancy chocolates gold-leafed with the vice-regal lion on them.

"Every guest must feel welcome," says Richard Legrand, Rideau Hall's longtime maître d'hôtel. "Every staff member must play an important role in welcoming, serving and hosting at Rideau Hall to make sure that from the moment the guests step in the front door until they leave, they're well taken care of, and when they leave, they leave with a good memory of their stay."

As well as using her husband's time in office to promote awareness of issues such as breast cancer, AIDS, substance abuse and Alzheimer's disease, Gerda Hnatyshyn took a strong personal interest in the historical preservation and restoration of Rideau Hall. Under her patronage and with

her support a volunteer group has been created to raise money for the acquisition of furniture, paintings and *objets d'art* of historical relevance to Rideau Hall.

Her other specific area of interest in the house came from her own background in dietetics and nutrition and her studies in cuisine in France: the menus (no one menu is ever repeated) and the service of food. The Rideau Hall kitchens prepare 70,000 servings a year. "Canadian products are used whenever possible. Specialties from all regions of the country such as New Brunswick fiddleheads and blueberries, Manitoba wild rice, Saskatoon berries, Western beef, lamb from Ontario, seafood from both coasts, and maple syrup produced on the grounds is often used in desserts."

Rideau Hall is our White House, our Buckingham Palace. It has heard the footsteps of our history marching through its doors and seems today to be more relevant than ever, unifying, encouraging, praising and rewarding those of us

*Rideau Hall chefs prepare
70,000 meals a year.*

who have done service for our country, establishing and maintaining traditions that make for a stronger national fabric.

As the Hnatyshyns have said, "It is fitting that Rideau Hall and the oldest portion of La Citadelle in Quebec City have been declared national historic sites because each has been the scene of important moments in Canadian history. Together they are Canada's living room, the places in which we welcome distinguished guests from all over the world and honour our own outstanding citizens."

Announcing the guests.

In the receiving line.

The governor general toasting the guest of honour.

AT HOME WITH

ALLISTER AND SUSAN MARSHALL

The orchard in blossom and at harvest time.

THE ANNAPOLIS VALLEY WAS FIRST SETTLED by the French in the early 1700s, and Allister Marshall still remembers people identifying orchards as having French origins, not by the particular apples they chose to grow, but by the way the trees were grouped in the orchard.

"The Annapolis Valley is a good place to grow apples because you have the north mountain on the one side to protect you from the Bay of Fundy and the wind and on the south you have a high plateau. This protection together with the good sandy soil allows a longer season for growing apples."

Allister, an agriculturist, expounds knowledgeably and lovingly on the place where he and his wife, Susan, came to live in 1964. They raised their children in this attractive clapboard house, built in 1840, "a typical valley house of the period with its frame window over the front door."

Their love of horses brought them together. As a young woman Susan trained for the National showjumping team, and Allister was also involved in showjumping, first as a rider and later as a competition judge.

His interest in horses began with his father, who he says was "dyed in the wool for horses." Of his private hunt and its eight couple of foxhounds, he declares, "There is no experience more stimulating than galloping across the countryside, wind to the fore, hounds in hot pursuit of their quarry." In the case of his hunt the scent is provided by a drag, not a live fox.

The breeding of horses and dogs is Susan's domain. The Marshalls' animal family consists of four horses, four Jack Russells and the hounds.

Allister is of Scottish Presbyterian descent. His ancestors came from western Scotland, sailing to Canada on the

137

Before the hunting season, Allister must exercise the hounds.

Allister returning to the barn after evening chores.

A cup of tea in the late afternoon is a daily ritual.

Lovely Nellie in 1755. They have spawned at least two men of the cloth for the Presbyterian church, but Allister's father was a lumber-mill owner whose mill prepared timbers for the barges used in the Normandy landings during the Second World War.

Susan is a descendant of the Oland brewing family. Her great-great-grandfather John Dunn Oland and his wife, Susannah, came from England in the late 1860s and started a family brewing business in the backyard of their home in Dartmouth, later moving to Halifax where the family fortunes flourished.

Susan describes her house as having comfortable, old-fashioned charm. It is filled with antiques, many inherited, others collected with infinite care and interest in the work of the early cabinet-makers of Nova Scotia and New Brunswick, such as C.S. Nesbitt. A pair of sixteenth-century chairs that stand in the hallway are part of a legacy of Susan's Spanish grandmother, Herlinda de Bedia y Martel, the daughter of a Spanish colonel who fought against the Americans in the Spanish-American war of 1898, and settled afterwards with his family in Cuba. He decided to send his daughters to school in Halifax as it was the nearest non-American centre for education. At Mount St. Vincent's Academy, Herlinda made friends with the Oland sisters, and on a visit to the convent with his mother their brother Sydney caught a glimpse of a beautiful Spanish girl with dark eyes. He instantly fell in love, but she was only seventeen at the

With two of the Jack Russells
she breeds, Susan sits in the
living room surrounded by some
of her favourite things.

A portrait of Susan's father
hangs in the dining room.

One of the pair of sixteenth-
century chairs Susan inherited
from her Spanish grandmother.

A portrait of Churchill hangs
above the riding boots in the
family sitting room.

time and they had to wait two years to become engaged. The marriage took place with great ceremony in the Cathedral of Mercidad in Havana.

In contrast to their colourful family histories, Susan and Allister's lives are firmly rooted in the land. The seventy acres of orchard were replanted by Allister in 1964. Applewood Farm is one of the largest commercial growers in the area, and as chairman of the board of Scotia Gold Co-operative Allister takes an active part in the apple-growing industry.

Allister and Susan see their role in the valley not as owners, but as guardians of the land they live on, and they treasure their affinity "with those who went before by planting hundreds of trees to shade the generations to come."

141

At Home With Rosalie and Isadore Sharp

"For one week in October, when the maple trees turn scarlet, we share meals with our children and their children in the sukkah to give thanks to God for our blessings," says Rosalie Sharp. Sukkot, the celebration of the harvest festival, is a much-valued tradition in the Sharp family. Historically, a sukkah was a tent or hut used by Israelites during their forty years of wandering in the desert in search of the Promised Land. Rosalie's sukkah is best described as an elegant conservatory floating among the trees of a hidden ravine in downtown Toronto.

The rituals of Sukkot are shared by the entire family. Rosalie tries to preserve for her grandchildren memories of her mother's family's sukkah in Ozorow, Poland. Imaginative strings of pine cones and chestnuts, together with boughs of maple and branches of willow, are hung from the ceiling, and Rosalie encourages the little ones to add their home-made decorations, so paper cut-outs and golden stars of David abound.

The table is covered with a patterned cloth of a rich purple and cyclamen hue. Along with the usual accoutrements, it is laid with the symbols of the ritual — candles, bread,

Rosalie shares a moment in the garden with her granddaughters.

The conservatory.

wine and honey. Also placed on the table are the *Lulav*, a branch of a palm tree bound together with leaves from three myrtles and two willows, each one representing a facet of human nature, and the *Etrog*, a yellow citron fruit which symbolizes the heart of human nature. At approximately 5:30 p.m. Rosalie and her granddaughters Julie and Erin light the candles, and the family gathers around while "Papa Max," Isadore's father, makes the blessing over the wine, the *Kiddush*, and the blessing over the bread, the *Ha'motzei*, and gives thanks to God for the joys of everyday life and for the benefits of the harvest. Then four generations of the family share a simple dinner of chicken soup and pasta. After dinner Papa Max challenges his grandson to a game of chess, closely observed by his son and great-grandson.

Rosalie, Julie and Erin light the candles and sing a prayer.

At Rosalie and Isadore's Sukkot, there's a discussion about the relevance of a sukkah in today's world. Rosalie suggests that it reminds us of our folly in believing that substantial houses filled with treasures can defend us against death or the unexpected. "The sukkah teaches us that builders of houses should be able to give them up or move out if

144

necessary, for renunciation is the secret of mastery." The weeklong ritual explores the practicability of Judaism, the affirmation of the holiness of pleasure and the gap between an imperfect world and a world redeemed.

Papa Max was born in Auschwitz, Poland in 1900. As a young man, he left Poland for Palestine, where he spent five years working as a pioneer helping to build the embryonic Zionist state. In 1925 he came to Canada and quickly established a reputation as a carpenter and builder of houses.

When Izzy Sharp left university he joined his father's small construction company as an architect. In 1961, he went into the hotel business with the Four Seasons Motel on Jarvis Street. Today he heads a chain that spans five continents. It is a strange irony of fate that while his son conquers the world through business, Max has never had any desire to return to the country of his birth. He has lived in Canada for seventy-five years and says he would never leave. "In Canada there are no wars, no worries, no problems. It is a peaceful place." Basking in the light of the candles, one can believe it for a while.

"Papa Max" makes the blessing over the bread and wine.

Four generations around the table.

OVERLEAF: A spirited chess game after dinner.

145

THE DUN-COLOURED FIELDS stretch unbroken almost as far as the eye can see, and the big sky of the Prairie landscape promises an early snow. Inside a machine shed, Don Cross, the patriarch of Bar Pipe Farms, welcomes the crowd of buyers to his fortieth annual sale of purebred Herefords.

In the last few days, the machine shed has been turned into an auction ring, with ribbons and pennants of past champions lining the walls. Forty-five bull calves and forty-five bred heifers are to be offered for sale in what is the culmination of a year's efforts, beginning with calving in February. Don and his wife, Shan, are both numb with anxiety on the most important day of the year at the ranch.

The cold November weather is quickly forgotten in the excitement and energy of the packed shed. Cowboy boots, jeans, Stetsons and warm down jackets are the order of the day, the bright colours in stark contrast to the plain home-made black clothes and hats of the Mennonite farmers sitting together at one side of the sales ring.

While Don stands beside the auctioneer, his sister Nan records each sale, a gruelling task as each animal is only in the ring for two minutes. One of Shan and Don's four children, Jay, a research scientist in Toronto, and their son-in-law, Bob, an oilman investment manager in Calgary, are in the pens outside sorting the animals for the auction ring. Shan stands in the lunch room behind the ring, greeting the buyers, usually by name — for most of them the Cross Hereford sale is an annual pilgrimage, and they come from all parts of the Canadian and American West and as far away as Australia.

For Shan, auction day involves looking after a full main house and a guest-house occupied by family, friends and buyers. An avid cook, she says she hates to serve "anything but beef when it is your business." Dinner before the auction may be meat loaf, macaroni and cheese, cole slaw and trifle. The menu at the party after the auction is traditional; the spiced beef is an old family recipe which Don's father used to make himself in huge crocks. It is still made the same way today and is absolutely delicious. An old friend who makes his own knives carves it paper-thin and guests eat it on buttered bread with Shan's mustard sauce. Home-

made soup, an open bar and Shan's ginger-snaps complete the meal.

As a young man, Don worked in his family's brewery in Calgary, but in 1962 he and Shan left the city behind and moved to the ranch, which had belonged to Don's father. The Bar Pipe brand was an old one made, but never used, by A.E. Cross, who came here from Montreal in 1870.

Shan says, "The ranch is Don's heritage, a family tradition and a business. It is a contagious way of life out here. The forebears that did come really came in those carts and it was tough, tough sledding. Everyone's accepted, there is no establishment and people in Calgary are participants more than spectators." The Cross family have been

A family portrait.

The foothills of the Rocky Mountains rise on the horizon of the Bar Pipe ranch.

Many people from far and wide, including local Mennonites, come to the annual Cross auction.

Cattle in the chute waiting their turn in the ring.

involved with the Calgary Stampede since the days of A.E. Cross, who was one of its four founders, and both Don and his father have been presidents. Don started out as a volunteer timer in the rodeo events the year he was married.

The Crosses have always taken great pleasure in welcoming visitors from around the world. According to Shan, "One of the largest and most festive parties took place in 1976 when we entertained breeders from twenty countries attending the World Hereford Congress in Calgary and the family had great fun when we put on a private branding for Prince Andrew."

At the end of auction day, Don and Shan appear more relaxed, and one understands when Shan says that "home is the focal point of our personal lives and the soul of the family. It is the constant in a changing world for all things familiar and familial, a place for friends, celebrations, memories, retreat and comfort."

The maintenance shed is transformed every year into an auction ring.

Bidding is serious business.

Don's sister Nan records the winning bid, and a friend's son rushes the receipts to the successful bidder.

AT
HOME
WITH

TRISHA
ROMANCE
AND
GARY
PETERSON

A Christmas afternoon sleigh ride with the children.

ARTIST TRISHA ROMANCE and her husband, Gary Peterson, who manages her business, live with their three children in a graceful nineteenth-century Georgian brick house set amidst four hectares of gardens and pastures in Niagara-on-the-Lake. "This house," Trisha says, "was love at first sight. I knew when I saw it that this is where I would raise my children and work." The stables were the final selling point, as she had always wanted a horse. Buying the house, at the time a huge financial burden for her and Gary, was the beginning of a love affair that has inspired much of her work. "Every house I have ever lived in has been the source of my work. I paint the little everyday occasions."

In fact the house's nostalgic charm and style mirror her paintings. She has renovated and decorated relentlessly, designing and painting furniture and wall friezes, creating *trompe-l'oeil* effects, dying upholstery fabric, drawing plans for the curtains and swags and pelmets for the curtain-maker and imbuing the house with the scent of log fires, warmed apple cider and potpourri from her garden.

On the first of October, Trisha starts playing Christmas carols, but secretly, because Gary thinks she is crazy to be so obsessed with Christmas so early. "I'm a Christmas person. Thoughts of Christmas are what get me through the fall after the frost has killed my garden." She has vivid memories of her childhood Christmases and today those memories inspire her own Christmas traditions. "Bells, the sound of sleigh-bells to me mean Christmas. My mother used to have sleigh-bells hanging on her back door and when as a child I heard them ringing in the wind, it meant that I had come home."

In the first week of December, work begins in earnest. Fresh green boughs hung with ropes, fruit and holly from her garden decorate mantels and doorways. Small lights are strung on the oaks outside. Old-fashioned burgundy-coloured bows are tied on the gateposts; a gingerbread house, a model of her own house, is assembled; and finally around December 15, her youngest child, Whitney, who is the other Christmas person in the house, helps her decorate the two Christmas trees. The smaller of the two is put up in the sun room, the Nativity scene carefully set out at its feet. The other tree, which is fourteen feet high, stands in the elbow of the main staircase, covered with lights and chandelier

prisms that Trisha discovered in a box in the attic when she moved in. Elves, angels and Santa Clauses are to be found in various guises, hanging on the trees, sitting on mantels, decorating tables, and peering out of birdcages. A frightening childhood illness gave her a strong belief in the protective spirit of angels and a yearning for the winged freedom of elves and fairies. It is all part of the rather magical and whimsical ambiance she creates around her.

On Christmas Eve, home from church, once the children have gone to bed, it is a special time for Trisha and Gary. He stuffs the stockings with what small treasures and jokes he has bought. He hooks them to the mantel in the sun room, she finishes wrapping the presents, they write a note from Santa and get to bed very late.

Christmas morning, the presents are opened amid the usual excitement and happy chaos. Around noon they eat brunch and finally grandparents, aunts, uncles and cousins arrive to help cook Christmas dinner, which is traditionally

Whitney, "the other Christmas person" in the family, has decorated her doll's house for the season.

In the master bedroom, which she stencilled and painted herself, Trisha hangs cedar boughs.

Trisha at work in her top-floor studio.

157

a baked ham with a mustard glaze. Trisha's mother makes her famous mashed potatoes, one sister makes apple pies, the other sister brings cookies. Trisha herself makes a hazelnut torte and a trifle of blueberries, peaches and raspberries, home-made custard and almond pound cake.

She decorates the dining-room table with holly, fresh evergreen boughs, angels and elves, lots of candles, hangs bells on the ends of the curtain tassels and lights the fire. The room glitters and glows with diffuse light and warmth. The children are the stars of this family celebration.

Art and life certainly imitate one another. In the hands of Trisha Romance, the candlelit rooms, the crackling fires, the pungent scent of evergreen boughs and the traditions of Christmas itself all create a bit of magic.